ELVINA PEARCE
ADVENTURES IN STYLE-BOOK 2
10 Original Piano Solos

These pieces offer refreshing and exciting repertoire that motivates students to excel, offers a variety a styles and keys, and presents music in five-finger positions with extensions that move in many octaves around the keyboard. Here is innovative repertoire that utilizes pedal to help create big sounds. The descriptive titles are designed to capture the imagination and nurture interpretive skills. The pieces sound harder than they are and will give students a profound sense of accomplishment.

CONTENTS

Editor: GAIL LEW
Production Coordinator: SHERYL ROSE
Art Design: MARTHA RAMIREZ

© 2002 BELWIN-MILLS PUBLISHING CORP. (ASCAP)
All Rights Administered by WARNER BROS. PUBLICATIONS U.S. INC.
All Rights Reserved including Public Performance for Profit

Peaceful Valley

ELVINA PEARCE

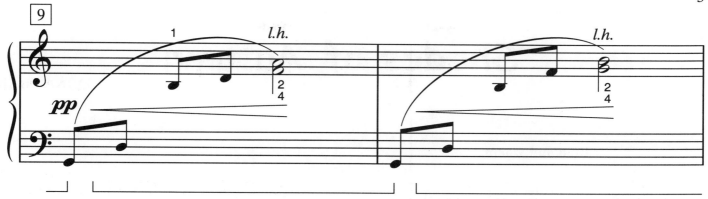

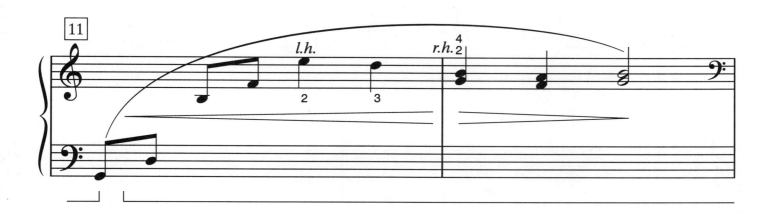

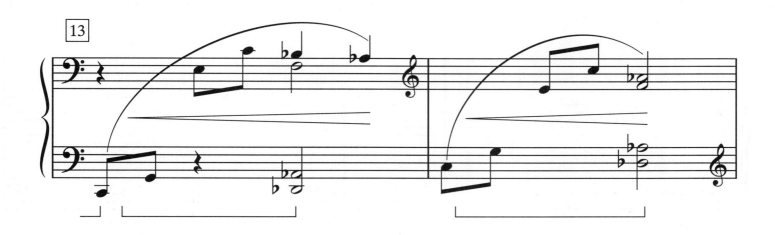

Shades of Autumn

ELVINA PEARCE

Memories

ELVINA PEARCE

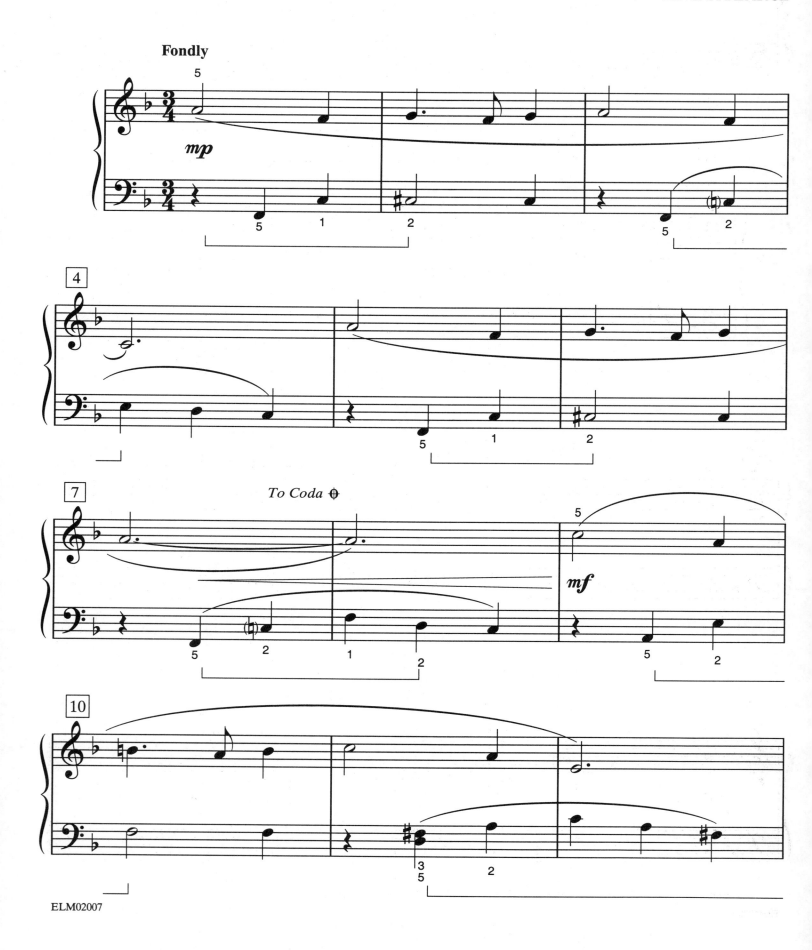

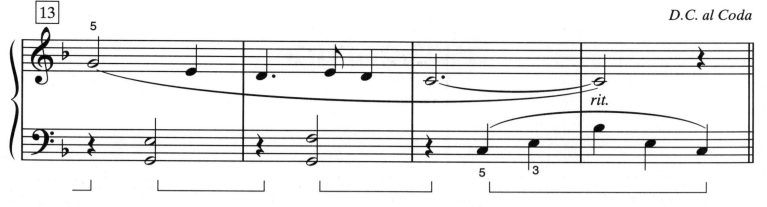

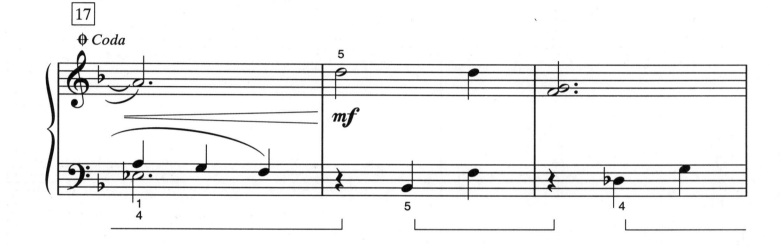

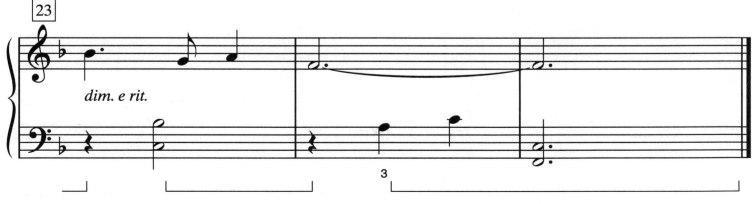

ELM02007

Swing Tune

ELVINA PEARCE

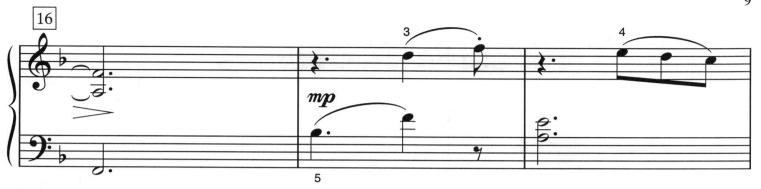

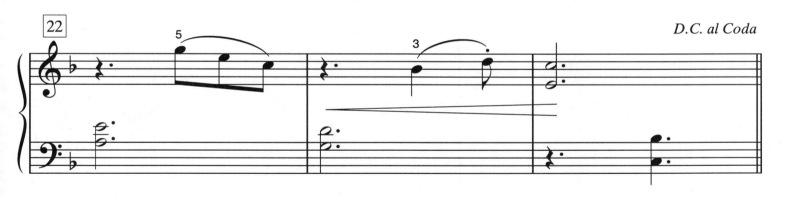

Fireside Memories

ELVINA PEARCE

Slowly and tenderly

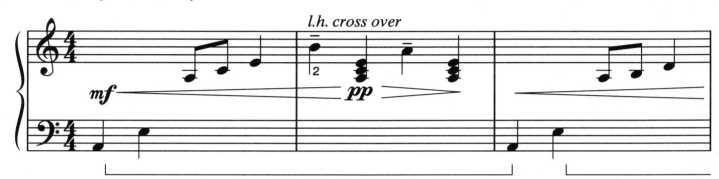

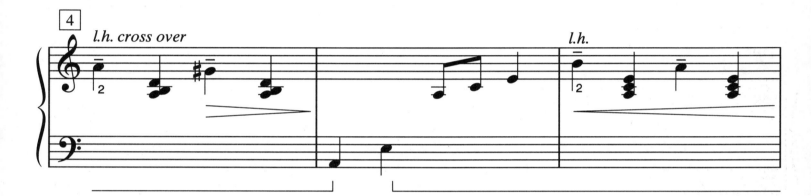

Skeleton Scamper

ELVINA PEARCE

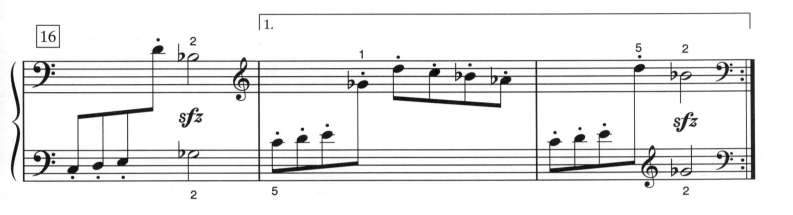

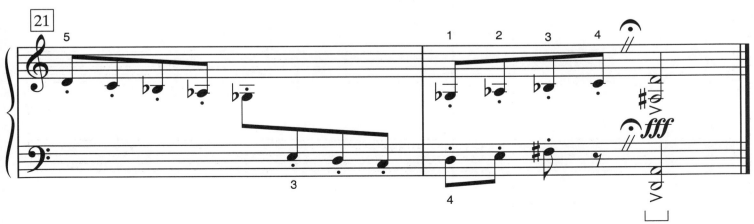

ELM02007

Jackhammer Blues

ELVINA PEARCE

Much energy but not fast!

staccato simile

Festival in Spain

ELVINA PEARCE

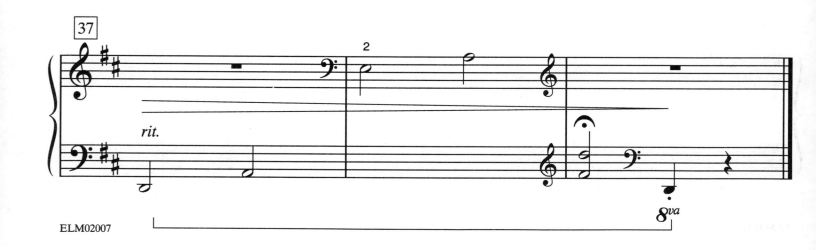

Tahitian Tango

ELVINA PEARCE

Magic Moments

ELVINA PEARCE

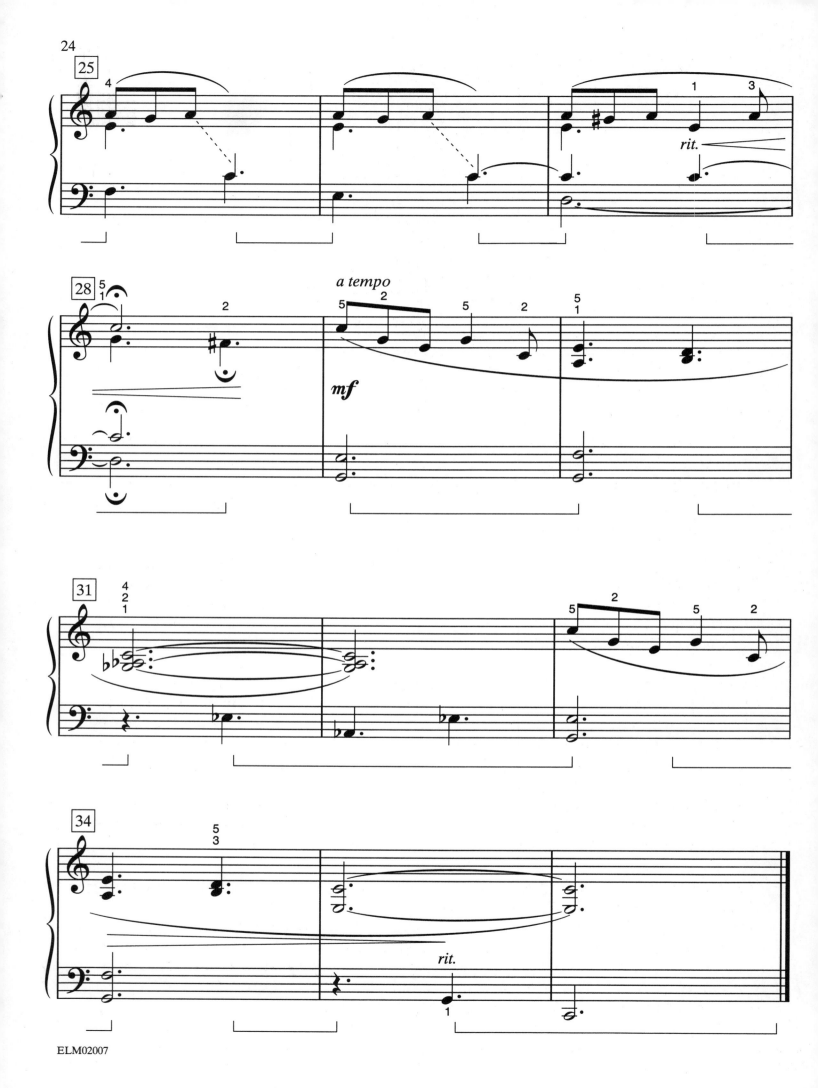